First published 2008

The Educational Company of Ireland
Ballymount Road
Walkinstown
Dublin 12

A trading unit of the Smurfit Kappa Group

The paper used in this book comes from Managed Forests in Northern Europe. For every tree felled, at least one new tree is planted

Co-ordinator: Frank Fahy
Artists: Kim Shaw, Kate Shannon
Design and Layout: The Design House
Printed in Ireland by: Colorman (Ireland) Ltd.

1 2 3 4 5 6 7 8 9
Acknowledgements
Photographs are courtesy of Alamy, Corbis, Kevin Dwyer,
Photocall Ireland and Shutterstock.

Please note that the information in the panels Fast Fact! and Over to You! and the listing of objectives at the bottom of the pages are not intended to be read by the pupils. These panels contain extra information that may be used by teachers or parents or may serve as oral language discussion cues.

Further information on each chapter is provided in the Teacher's Resource Book.

The Web References on page 96 are intended as a guide for teachers. At the time of going to press, these web addresses were active and contained some information relevant to the topics in this book. However, The Educational Company of Ireland and the authors do not accept responsibility for the views or information contained in these websites. Content and addresses can change outside of our control. It is important that children are supervised when investigating websites.

Contents

All About Me!

A - Draw or glue a picture of yourself in the photo frame.

B - Write about yourself.

name	age	years	birthday	live
brothers	sisters	family	class	friend

My name is _____.

_____

_____

_____

_____

_____

4

Children become aware of change and continuity through exploring growth, change and development in their own lives.

C - Let's talk!

Jack as a baby.

Jack today.

D - Draw

Jack has changed since he was a baby. So have you!
Draw two things that you can do now, that you could
not do when you were a baby.

Be Healthy!

The school soccer team needs a new player. You must decide between Fit Fred and Lazy Larry. Think carefully before you decide.

Fit Fred

Hi! My name is Fit Fred. I want to be a famous footballer when I grow up. I really take care of my body.

Favourite Food
I love fruit. Apples are my favourite.

Favourite Drink
I drink lots of water, juice and milk.

Favourite Hobbies
I love football and swimming.

Lazy Larry

Hello! My name is Lazy Larry. I play football every day – but only on my computer. I hate running and love being lazy!

Favourite Food
Crisps and biscuits.

Favourite Drink
I hate milk. Water is boring. I prefer cola.

Favourite Hobbies
Watching TV or playing computer games.

Children work scientifically to gain an understanding of the importance of food and exercise for their growth and development.

A - Draw the school team with the new player.

B - Let's talk!

1. Do you think Fit Fred is healthy? Why/Why not?

_____

2. Do you think Lazy Larry is healthy? Why/Why not?

_____

3. What can you do to make sure you keep your body healthy?

_____

C - My Fact File

Name
_____
Age
_____
Class
_____
Favourite Food
_____
Favourite Drink
_____
Favourite Hobbies
_____

D - My Picture

Sport is Fun

This is Pat.
He is our football coach.
He trains us every Saturday.
We have great fun.
Pat is our hero!

This is Lisa.
She is our swimming coach.
We dive, swim and play in the pool. We have a splashing time!

Remember there is no 'I' in TEAM. We must all work together.

It is great to win but sometimes we lose. Just go out there and do your best.

Children recognise and appreciate the interdependence of people in their local community.

A - Questions

1 Who is the football coach?_____
_____

2 On what day does Pat train?_____
_____

3 Who is their hero?_____

4 Who is Lisa?_____

5 What do the children do in the pool?_____
_____

6 Do the children work together?_____
_____

B - My favourite team

My favourite team is called_____ .

The coach's name is_____ .

Draw your team jersey.

Front	Back

C - Let's talk!

Talk about the special olympics or famous sports people.

Communications – Old and New

A - Let's talk!

Look at the items in Set a.
Which item was invented first?
Write the number 1 beside this item.
Which item was invented next?
Write the number 2 beside this item and so on.
Now do the same for Set b.

Over to you!

Find out about the history of radio and television in Ireland. See www.rte.ie

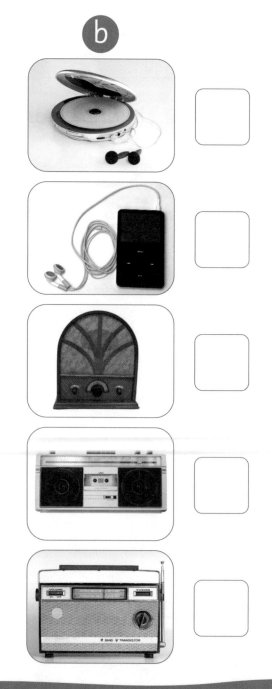

Children investigate the history of communications and compare old systems with modern technological innovations.

B - Look at these old items.

Draw the new models of each item.

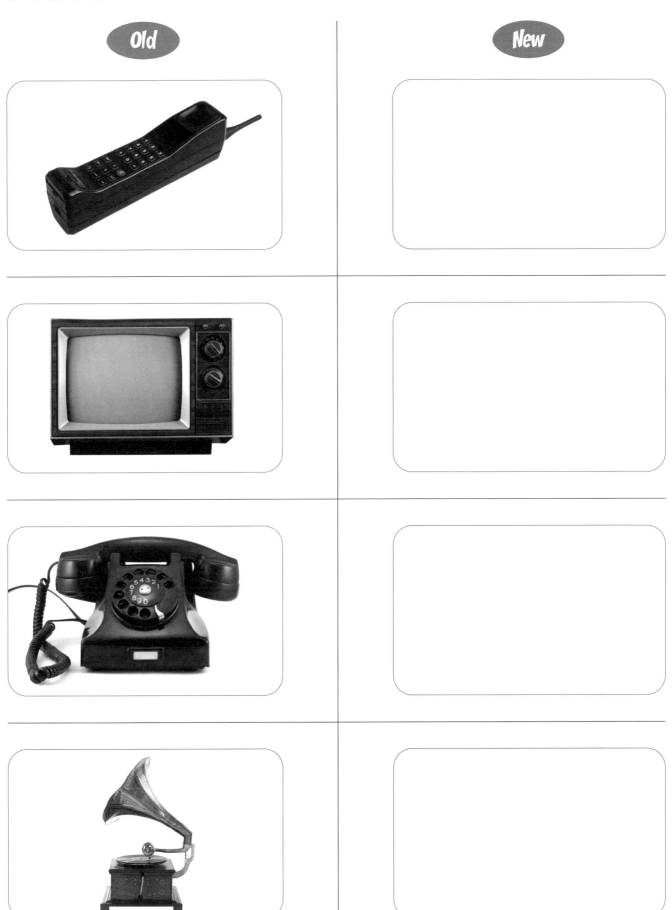

Good Food

Your body needs good food to grow strong.
To keep healthy you must eat more of some
foods and less of others. We use the Food Pyramid
to help us make healthy food choices.

The Food Pyramid

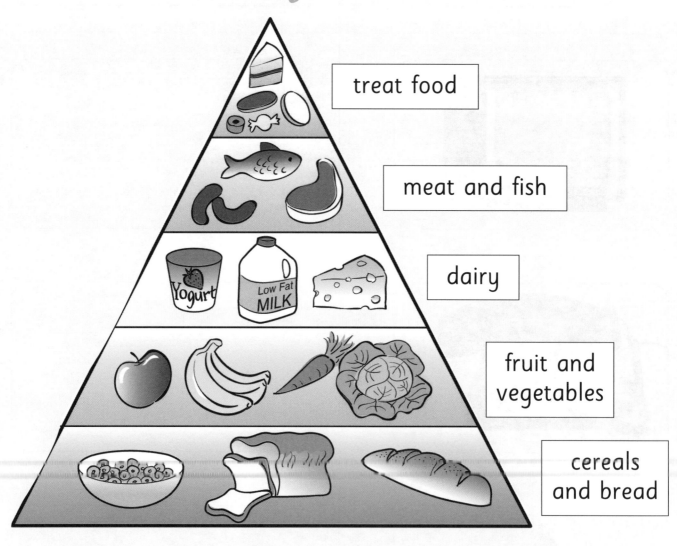

treat food

meat and fish

dairy

fruit and vegetables

cereals and bread

You should have three healthy meals every day
– breakfast, lunch and dinner.
Drinking lots of water is a very good idea too.

Children classify food in order to gain an understanding of a healthy balanced diet through familiarisation with the Food Pyramid.

A - Sort the food.

toast cornflakes chocolate cheese apple
chicken carrot sweets cod milk

Treat food	Meat and fish	Dairy

Fruit and vegetables	Cereals and bread

B - Draw a healthy lunch.

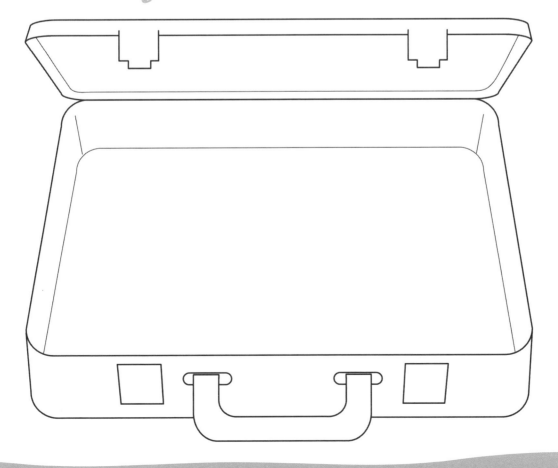

13

Houses in Far Away Places

We all live in different houses. Most of our houses are made from blocks or bricks. Not all houses are made from these.

Houses made of wood

In countries where there is a lot of snow in winter, houses are made of wood. Wood keeps the house very warm. Wooden shutters on the windows keep the heat in.

Mud houses

It is very hot in Africa. Some houses have thick mud walls and small windows. There is no roof. Branches of trees help to keep the sun off.

Tents

Some people live in tents in the desert. They have herds of goats and camels. There is very little grass in the desert. They are always on the move, looking for grass.

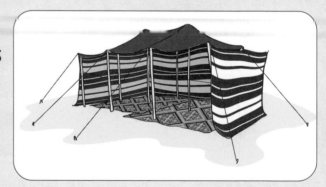

Children analyse homes in different countries and discuss the availability of raw materials in those areas.

Houses on stilts

In parts of Asia there is a lot of rain.
Often there are very bad floods.
Some people live in houses built on stilts.
The stilts help to keep the water out.

Igloo

People who live in the Arctic are called
Inuits. Some Inuits hunt for meat and
fish. They build a house called an igloo.
It is made from blocks of frozen snow.
The igloo gives shelter from the cold.

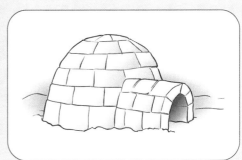

A - Write Yes or No.

1 Wooden houses are built where there is a lot of snow._____

2 Wood keeps the house very cold. _____

3 Houses in Africa have small windows._____

4 Some houses in Africa are made of mud. _____

5 Some people in the desert live in tents._____

6 Stilts help to keep the flood water out._____

7 Inuits live in Africa._____

8 An igloo is made from blocks of mud._____

B - Over to you!

Draw a picture of your home.
Draw a picture of a home from a faraway place.

Games from the Past

Grandad, what games did you play when you were a boy?

My friends and I loved to play with catapults, marbles and ring boards.

'We had catapults made from twigs and elastic. Whoever knocked over the most cans was the winner.'

'We put marbles into a circle. The winner hit the most marbles out of the circle.'

'Throwing rubber rings was great fun. Whoever got the highest score was the winner.'

Children become familiar with games from the past by interviewing an older person and recording games played.

A - Let's play with words.

1 We had catapults made of twigs and _____ (elastic, plastic, wool).

2 We put marbles into a _____ (box, square, circle).

3 The person who hit the most marbles out of the circle was the _____ (loser, best, winner).

4 The rings were made from _____ (wood, paper, rubber).

B - Games from the past

Ask an older person about a game they played when they were young. Write about it.

Name of the game: _____

How to play the game: _____

_____

_____

_____

_____

Draw the picture.

Push and Pull

A push or pull can make something move. Some things need a push to work and some things need a pull. Pushes and pulls are called forces. A strong push will make something move more than a gentle push.

A - Circle the pushes in red. Circle the pulls in blue.

B - Sam's Car

Sam has great fun racing his cars. He likes to make a ramp and see how far his car will go before it will stop. Help him to find the material that will make his car go the furthest.

Try using different materials and measure how far the car will travel on each one.

carpet

MATERIAL	Carpet	Wood	Bubblewrap	Cardboard
DISTANCE	_____ cm	_____ cm	_____ cm	_____ cm

C - The Results

Which material came 1st, 2nd, 3rd, and 4th?

1st_____

2nd_____

3rd_____

4th_____

Italy

Fast Facts!

The Romans made the first ice-lolly.
The number 17 is unlucky in Italy!
The word Ciao means Hello and Goodbye.
The smallest country in the world is Vatican City inside Rome.
There are about 350 different pasta shapes.

Ciao! (Hello)

My name is Mario. I am from Italy. People say my country looks like a boot! I live in a beautiful city called Venice. I go to school on a waterbus. When I grow up I want to own a gondola like my Dad. I would like to own a Ferrari but I would have no place to drive it!

This is the leaning tower of Pisa. It moves a little bit every year. My teacher says it will never fall over.

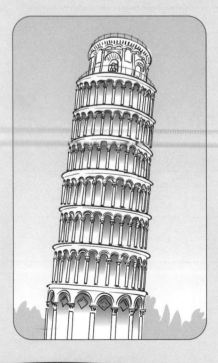

We have lots of ice-cream in Italy. We call it gelato. Did you know that pizza and pasta come from Italy? Pasta comes in many shapes. I like spaghetti best.

Using maps and globes, children develop an awareness of people and places in another European country and become familiar with some of the aspects of life there.

A - Fill in the correct word.

1 R_____ is the capital of Italy.

2 The leaning tower is in P_____.

3 V_____ is built on water.

4 AC Milan soccer team is based in M_____.

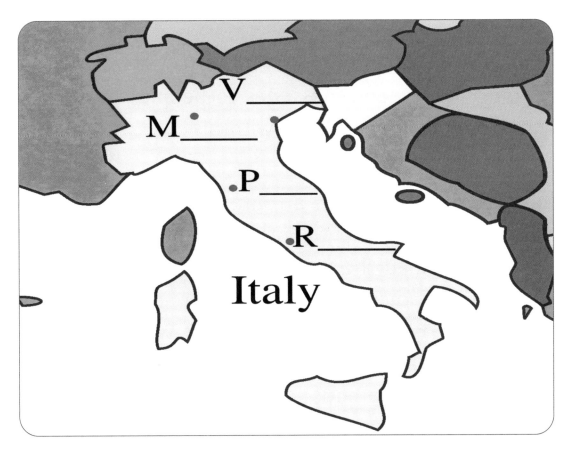

B - Wordsearch. Find these words in the Ferrari.

Venice gondola Ferrari Pisa pasta
pizza ice-cream waterbus Italy spaghetti

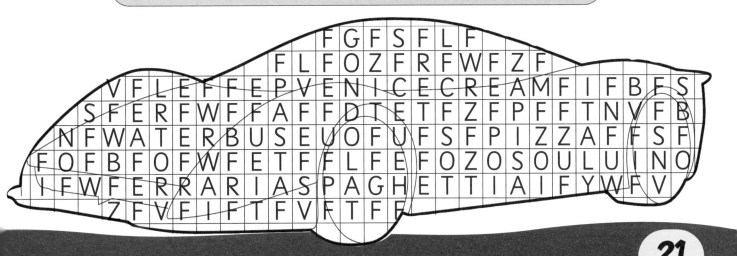

Alexander Graham Bell

Alexander Graham Bell was born in Scotland. When he grew up he went to America. He worked with people who found it hard to hear and speak.

Alexander was an inventor. He wanted to invent a machine to send messages to people far away. He worked very hard with his helper Mr Watson.

One day, Mr Watson was in a room with a machine. Alexander was in a different room with another machine. A line joined the two machines. Mr Watson heard Alexander's voice say, 'Mr Watson – come here – I want to see you.' These were the first words spoken on a 'telephone'. Alexander Graham Bell invented many things but he is most famous for inventing the telephone.

A - Questions

1 Where was Alexander Graham Bell born?

_____

2 Where did Alexander live when he grew up?

_____

3 What did Alexander want to invent?

_____

4 Who was Alexander's helper?

_____

5 What were the first words spoken on a telephone?

_____

Children explore and discuss Alexander Graham Bell's contribution to developments in the area of communication and technology.

B - Let's talk!

C - Pretend that you are Mr Watson.

What did you do or say when you heard Alexander's voice say:
'Mr Watson – come here – I want to see you'?

_____

_____

_____

_____

Discover Materials

Some materials are found in nature. We can get them from animals, plants or deep in the ground. Other materials are not found in nature. We have to make them. These are called man-made materials. There are many kinds of materials. They are all good at doing different jobs.

Fast Facts!

The strongest metal is Tungsten.

The first man-made plastic, 'celluloid', is said to have been shown by Alexander Parkes at an exhibition in London in 1862.

Metals

Metals are found in rocks deep in the ground. They are very strong. We use metals to build aeroplanes and bridges.

Plastics

Plastic is not a natural material. It is made from oil in special factories. Plastic is waterproof. We can use it to make wellies, raincoats and umbrellas.

Children sort and classify materials according to observable features and explore how and why they are used.

Glass

Glass is not a natural material. It is made from sand. We can see through glass. We use it to make windows.

Fabric

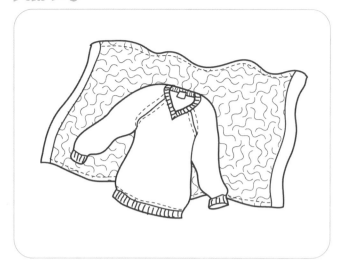

Some fabrics are natural (e.g., wool and leather). They come from animals. Others are man-made (e.g., nylon). We use fabrics to make clothes and blankets.

A - Say if these materials are natural or man-made.

_____

_____

_____

_____

_____

_____

Living in a Box

Have you ever played in a cardboard box? Have you ever pretended it was a boat, a car or even a jumbo jet? You can have great fun with a cardboard box.

Some people have no place to live. They have no homes. They have to live in a box or whatever they can find. They are very poor. They have no money for food. They have no money for a house. They need people to help them.

Tim

Ranja

This is Tim. He has no home. He lives in Dublin. Kind people bring him food and blankets.

This is Ranja. His family is very poor. They live in a hut. It is made out of plastic and bits of wood. This place is called a shantytown.

Children develop awareness of homelessness in Ireland and in faraway places.

A - Pretend that you are Ranja. Write your story.

My name is _____

_____

_____

_____

_____

B - Pretend that you are Tim. Write your story.

My name is _____

_____

_____

_____

_____

C - Draw some things that Ranja and Tim need to make life better for them.

Explore Materials

Jack has a new torch. He is having lots of fun playing with it. When he shines it at some materials he can see through them. They are **transparent**. When he shines it at other materials he cannot see through them. They are **opaque**.

A - Transparent or Opaque?

Find out if Jack was able to see through these materials. Are they transparent or opaque?

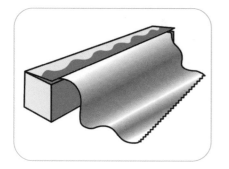

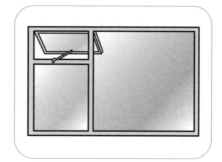

o _____   t _____   _____

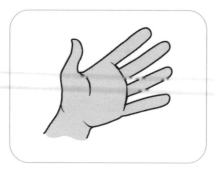

_____   _____   _____

Megan wants to make a boat to play with in the bath. She is not sure what materials to use. Some materials soak up water and get very wet. 'I don't want my boat to sink,' says Megan. 'I must make it waterproof.' Megan gets lots of different materials and tries to find the best one for her boat.

B - Waterproof Experiment

This is what Megan did to find the material for her boat.

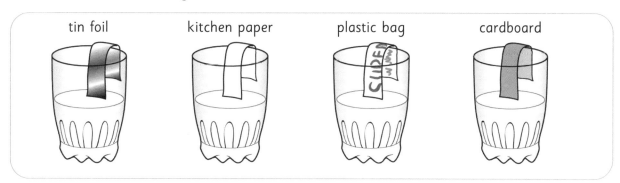

tin foil kitchen paper plastic bag cardboard

C - Questions

1 Which materials do you think Megan used? Why?

_____

2 Which materials did Megan not use? Why?

_____

3 Which material soaked up the most water?

_____

4 Which materials were waterproof?

_____

Family Treasures

Hello! My name is Hasibur.
I am nine years old. I am from Pakistan.
I live with my dad, mam, brother and sister.
My family moved to Ireland two years ago.

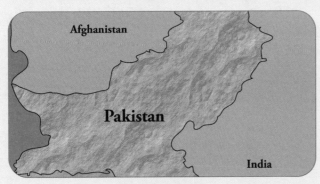

My dad works in a hotel.
My mam works at home.
When we moved from Pakistan,
we brought some special things
with us.

This is my family.

My dad brought his pipe called a 'hookah'. My mam brought spices for cooking. My sister brought a scarf called a 'dupatta', a tunic called a 'kamiz' and trousers called 'shalwar'. My brother brought books. We also brought our holy book. It is called the Koran.

Children work as historians by gathering and examining memorabilia from their own families and the families of others.

A - Questions

1. What country is Hasibur from?

   _____

2. Where does Hasibur's dad work?

   _____

3. What did Hasibur's mam bring to Ireland?

   _____

4. What did Hasibur's sister bring to Ireland?

   _____

5. What did Hasibur's brother bring to Ireland?

   _____

B - What do you see in the picture?

Write the words.

_____   _____   _____   _____

C - Make a list.

Make a list of special things you and your family would bring if you were moving to another country.

_____

_____

_____

_____

Planet Earth

Fast Fact!

Long ago people thought the earth was flat. They were afraid to sail too far from land in case they might fall off the edge!

The earth is like a huge ball. It is much, much bigger than you can imagine. If you walked all around the earth it would take longer than one year. You would need to walk all day and all night! We cannot see that the earth is like a ball. Only the astronauts in space can see that.

Planet Earth is covered with land and water. There is far more water than land.

After you sit in a beanbag you will see lots of humps and hollows. The earth is a bit like that. If you travel by aeroplane you can see them below. The humps are mountains and the hollows are valleys.

We share the earth with many, many people.
We live in different countries.
We look different.
We have different-coloured skin.
We speak different languages.
But we are all humans living on the same planet. All 5 billion of us!

Children develop familiarity with Planet Earth through questioning and observing.

A - Class Survey – Special Places

On the map, show places in Europe that are special to you.

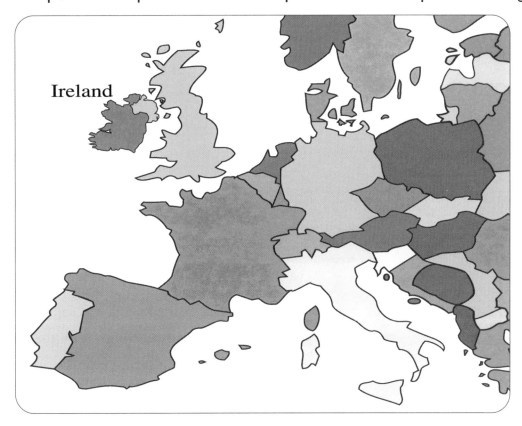

Ireland

B - What do you see in the picture?

Write the word.
Then write something you have learned about each one.

_____   _____   _____   _____

1 _____

2 _____

3 _____

4 _____

Heat and temperature

We use heat to cook, wash and keep ourselves warm.
A thermometer tells us how hot or cold something is.
It tells us the temperature. A high temperature means it is hot.
A low temperature means it is cold.

We measure temperature in degrees Celsius (°C).

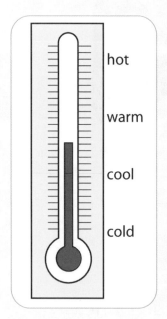

At 100°C
Water will boil at 100°C.

At 37°C
Our body temperature is 37°C.

At 0°C
Water will freeze at 0°C.

A - Measure the temperature.

Use a thermometer to measure the temperature in these places.

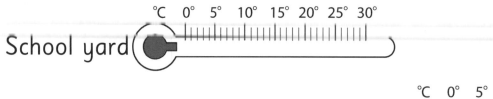

School yard

Inside the classroom

Children estimate temperature and measure it using a thermometer. They also explore and investigate ways of insulating.

Mark's Hot Chocolate

Some materials are good at keeping things warm. They stop the heat from getting out.

B - Experiment

Mark loves hot chocolate but it always goes cold too quickly. Help him to find the best material to keep it warm for longer.

a sock

tin foil

bubble wrap

kitchen paper

Predict

1. Which material do you think will work best? Why?

   _____

2. Which material do you think will not work well? Why?

   _____

The Results

Which material came 1st, 2nd, 3rd, and 4th?

1st_____

2nd_____

3rd_____

4th_____

_____ is the best material for keeping things warm.

Christmas Customs

Christmas is a happy time. Christ's birthday is celebrated in different ways in many countries. These ways are known as Christmas customs.

Christmas in The Philippines lasts for 22 days. On Christmas Eve, families have a midnight feast. Children visit their grannies and grandads on Christmas Day. The last day of Christmas is called 'The Feast of the Three Kings'.

Some children put their shoes outside so that the Kings will leave presents of money or sweets in them.

Many children in Mexico take part in a procession called a 'posada', the Spanish word for 'inn'. The children carry candles and clay statues of Mary and Joseph. They call to their friends' houses and sing.

They are told to leave because there is no room at the 'inn'. They call to a few houses until they find the 'inn'. Here they say prayers. After this, they have a party and watch fireworks.

Children explore and discuss the origins and traditions of Christmas and discuss customs and traditions in other lands.

A - Write the missing words.

1 Christmas lasts for _____ days in The Philippines.

2 The last day of Christmas in The Philippines is
The _____ of The Three_____ .

3 Many children in M_____take part in a
procession called a '_____'.

4 'Posada' is the S_____ word for '_____ '.

5 The children carry c_____ and clay statues of
M_____ and J_____ .

B - Write down some Christmas customs celebrated in Ireland.

Christmas tree   crib   candles   lights
decorations   presents   dinner   pudding

_____

_____

_____

_____

_____

_____

C - Draw a picture of one of these customs.

Arctic Weather

The top of the world

Have you ever heard of
the North Pole?
Sometimes it is called
'the top of the world'.
The land and water
around the North Pole
are called the Arctic.
It is very, very cold there.
There is ice and snow
all the time – even
in summer!

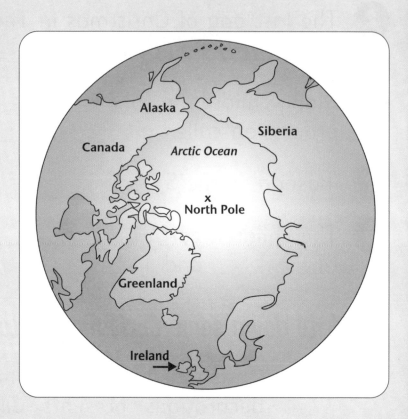

Whales, seals and many birds find lots of fish
to eat in the cold Arctic water. In winter most
of the birds fly to warmer countries. Some of
the animals hibernate.

Icebergs

An iceberg is like a mountain
of ice floating in the sea. It looks
very beautiful but it is very
dangerous to ships. About 100
years ago a big ship called the
Titanic was going from Cork
to America. It hit an iceberg.
It sank. Most of the people on
the ship drowned in the sea.

Children develop their geographical skills by exploring weather conditions in the Arctic.

A - Write Yes or No.

1. The North Pole is at the top of the world. _____
2. It is very hot at the North Pole. _____
3. Animals hibernate in summer. _____
4. Ireland is near the North Pole. _____
5. Greenland is near the North Pole. _____
6. An iceberg is an ice-cream. _____
7. Icebergs are dangerous. _____
8. The Titanic is in America. _____

B - Show the North Pole on the globe.

C - Join the dots. Colour.

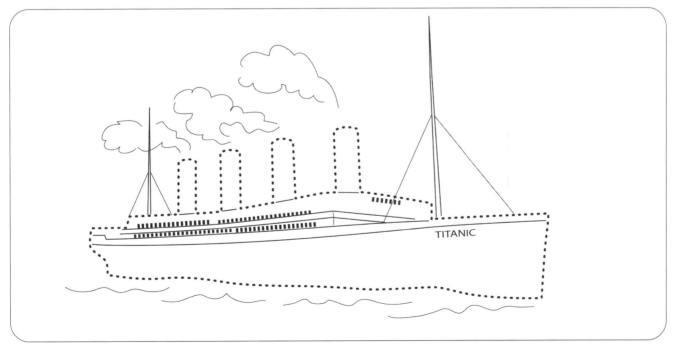

TITANIC

Shopping Tales

Hello! I'm Tim. We live near the shop. Sometimes I go to the shop to buy milk and bread. At the weekends, we go in the car to the shopping centre. There is a big supermarket in the shopping centre. There are lots of smaller shops. We buy meat, vegetables and lots of food in the supermarket.

Hello! I am Tim's mammy. When I was a small girl, there was no shopping centre in the town. There was a small supermarket. My family got some food in the supermarket. My mammy got meat at the butcher's shop. She got bread at the bakery.

Hello! I am Tim's grandad. Shops were very small when I was a boy. We had no car. My mammy walked or cycled to the shops every day to buy fresh bread, milk and meat. There were no trolleys or tills in the shops.

Children explore and become aware of continuity and change in their environment through the medium of commercial and retail outlets.

A - Let's talk!

Look at the photographs. Discuss.

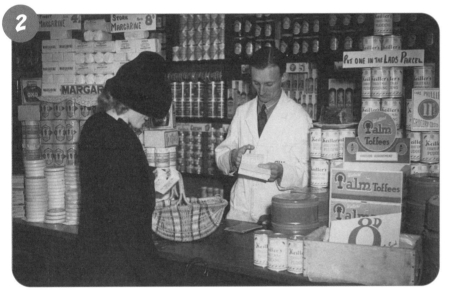

Fast Fact!

In 2001, Ireland used 1.2 billion plastic bags. A tax on plastic bags, introduced in 2002, reduced this number by 90%.

B - This is a shopping list from long ago.

Bread
Eggs
Jam
Flour
Milk
Tea

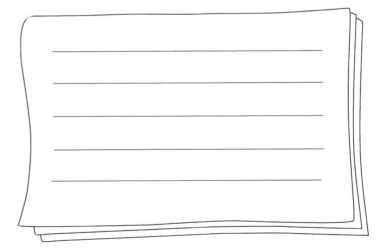

Write what you would put on your shopping list.

Electricity

Would you like to learn some magic tricks? These tricks will amaze your friends!

Jumping Paper

Tear some paper into small pieces. Rub a plastic comb through your hair. Hold the comb over the paper and watch the pieces jump!

Balloon Fun

Blow up a balloon. Rub it against a woolly jumper. Gently press the balloon against a wall and watch it stick!

Bending Water

Turn on a tap and let water flow gently. Rub a plastic comb through your hair. Hold the comb near the water and watch the water bend!

Fast Fact!

These tricks use **static electricity** to work.
It is made when you rub some things together.
We use electricity every day for light and heat.
Electricity is very helpful.

Children become aware of the uses and dangers of electricity. They work scientifically to examine the effects of static electricity.

A - Colour the things that use electricity in the kitchen.

B - Let's talk!

Electricity can also be very dangerous. We must be very careful around things that use electricity.
What are these children doing that is dangerous?

Arctic Animals

Fast Fact!

All polar bears are left-handed!

Hello! I'm Annie the Arctic fox.
I use my nose to find my dinner.
In summer my coat is grey or brown.
In winter it is white.
Can you guess why?

Hello! I'm Norman Narwhal.
I live in the cold Arctic water.
I love fish.
My front tooth sticks out like a spike.
It is about three metres long.
(That's more than twice your height.)

Hello! I'm Rosie the Ringed Seal.
I swim for a long time under water.
Then I come up for air.
If I cannot find a hole I bang the ice
with my head to make one.

Hello! I'm Peter Polar Bear.
Hunters find it hard to see me
in the snow. My fur and my fat
keep me warm in winter.
I like to eat seals.
Look out Rosie!

Children explore and analyse animals from a different habitat.

A - Questions

1 What colour is the Arctic fox in winter?

_____

2 What colour is the Arctic fox in summer?

_____

3 Where do narwhals live?

_____

4 How long is the narwhal's front tooth?

_____

5 Can ringed seals swim?

_____

6 How does the seal make a hole in the ice?

_____

7 What keeps the polar bear warm in winter?

_____

8 What do polar bears eat?

_____

B - Write about your favourite Arctic animal.

 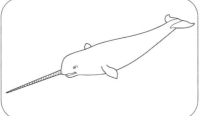  

My favourite Arctic animal is _____

_____

_____

Families in the Past

'Life was different when I was your age,'
said Granny. 'I walked to school every day.

We had no car. After school I had lots of jobs
to do, like washing, cleaning and cooking.
When I finished my homework I read a book
or played with my dolls.

We had no television. There were no computers,
DVDs or CDs then. I played hopscotch, skipping
games and chasing with my friends.

I went to the shops on my bicycle for my mam.
Sometimes, I got sweets. Toffees were my favourite!'

Children work as historians by interviewing and recording aspects of an older person's life.

A - Interview an older person. Ask the questions and write the answers.

1. Where did you live?_____

2. How many brothers and sisters did you have?

   Brothers_____ Sisters_____

3. Did your family have a car?_____

4. Did your family have a television?_____

5. What was your favourite treat?_____

6. How did you go to school?_____

7. What was your favourite subject?_____

8. What games did you play with your friends?_____

   _____

   Write two more questions you would like to ask:

9. _____

10. _____

B - Pretend that you live in the past. Draw a picture.

Going Outside

It is a lovely sunny day. Miss Greene and her class are going outside to study a habitat. They are going to the school garden.

Miss Greene warns the children to be careful and not to harm any plant or animal.

All the children are excited. They use different ways to explore the plants and animals in the habitat.

A - Let's talk!

The children find lots of flowers and see many minibeasts. They make drawings of everything they see so that they can learn more about them in the classroom.

Children observe and identify a variety of living things in their local environment. They record and classify their findings.

Our Class Field Trip

Minibeasts

Draw	Name	How many?

Plants

Draw	Name	How many?

Making Maps

Fast Fact!

The first maps were made more than 4,000 years ago.

Maps are pictures of places as they are seen from above. Maps help us to find our way from place to place. We can use pictures instead of words to make maps.

traffic lights   roundabout   bridge   farm   school   church

Garda Station   hospital   supermarket   park   playground   fire station

A - Let's talk!

John lives in the town. Talk about all the things he sees on his way to school.

Children's map-reading skills are developed through exploring maps and learning about directions.

B - What do you see on your way to school?

I see _____

_____

_____

Giving directions

We can say, 'Go right, go left, go straight on'.
This is called 'giving directions'.
We can also say, 'Go north, go south, go east,
go west'.

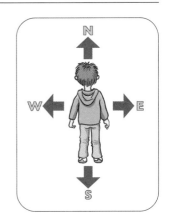

C - Fill in the gaps. Colour the map.

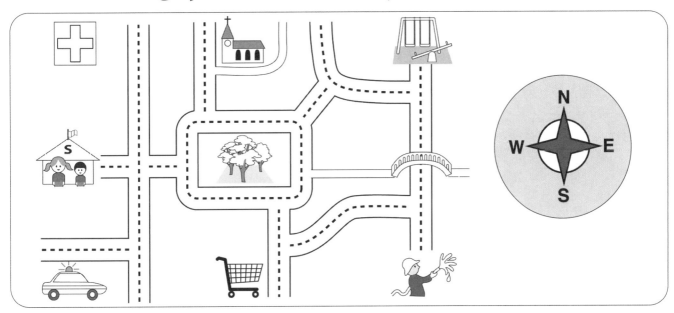

1 The_____ is north of the park.

2 The_____ is east of the park.

3 The_____ is south of the park.

4 The_____ is west of the park.

5 The hospital is_____ of the church.

6 The fire station is_____ of the supermarket.

7 The playground is_____ of the bridge.

8 The Garda Station is_____ of the school.

The Brown Bull of Cooley

'I am richer!'

'I am richer than you!'

Long ago, Queen Maeve and her husband Ailill lived in Connacht.
One day, they had a row.

They sent their servants to count everything they owned. They both had the same amount of riches except for one thing. Ailill owned a strong white bull and Queen Maeve had none. Queen Maeve was very jealous.

She sent her messengers to Cooley in Ulster for a big brown bull. A man called Daire owned the bull. Daire did not want to give her the bull. Queen Maeve sent her army to fight for the bull. There was a big battle. Queen Maeve took the brown bull back to Connacht.

The brown bull and Ailill's white bull had a fight. The white bull died. The brown bull ran all the way back to Cooley.
It was very tired and it fell down dead.
That was the end of the brown bull of Cooley.

Children listen to, discuss and re-tell an Irish legend. They communicate the events of the legend through the medium of writing and drama.

A - Questions

1 Where did Queen Maeve and Ailill live?

_____

2 Why was Queen Maeve very jealous of Ailill?

_____

3 Who owned the brown bull of Cooley?

_____

4 What happened to Ailill's white bull?

_____

5 Did Queen Maeve keep the brown bull of Cooley? Why?

_____

B - Colour the picture. Talk about it.

C - Write three sentences using these words.

Queen Maeve   servants   battle

1 _____

2 _____

3 _____

Our Feathered Friends

The cuckoo

The cuckoo is a lazy bird. She lays an egg in another bird's nest. The other bird takes care of it.

The young cuckoo is mean. It throws all the other eggs out of the nest so it can have all the food!

The robin

The robin does not like other birds to visit its space. It will get cross and stick out its little red breast while singing a 'stay away' song. The robin likes eating worms and insects.

The blackbird

The blackbird has lovely black feathers and a yellow beak. It has yellow rings around its eyes too. It sings a nice loud song. Worms and insects are its favourite dinner.

Feeding birds

Birds find it hard to find food to eat in winter. A bird table in the garden can help them. Put some seeds and nuts on the table for the birds. You will be able to watch all the birds that will come to visit.

Children observe, analyse and record a variety of common garden birds in their local environment.

A - Join the dots. Colour.

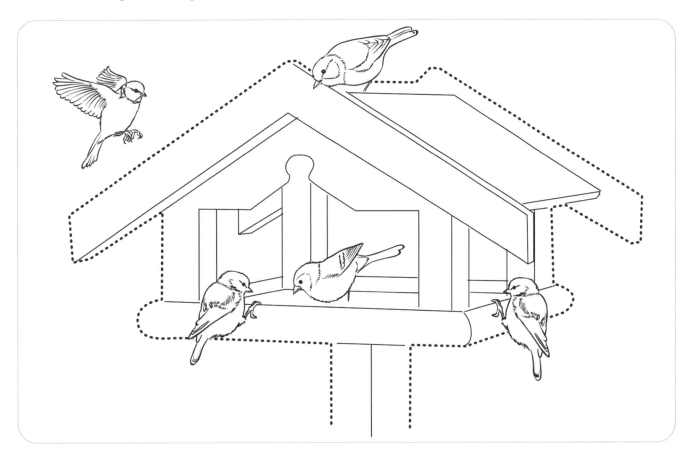

B - Questions

1. Where does the cuckoo lay her eggs?

   _____

2. In what way is the young cuckoo mean?

   _____

3. What does the robin do when it is cross?

   _____

4. What colour beak does the blackbird have?

   _____

5. What does the blackbird like to eat?

   _____

6. Why is it a good idea to have a bird table?

   _____

The Land Down Under

Australia is an island. It is about 100 times the size of Ireland. A big part of Australia is desert. It is very hot and very dry. Most of the people live near the sea because it is cooler.

Meet Mildred

This is Mildred. She is aborigine. She lives in Australia. Mildred's dad plays the didjeridu.

Living in the outback

Some people live in the outback. The outback is huge. Schools are so far away that children do not go there. They talk to the teacher on a radio instead. If you are sick in the outback the Flying Doctor comes to help.

Kangaroos and Koalas

A kangaroo can hop very fast. The baby kangaroo is called a joey.

A koala is like a cuddly teddy bear. The baby stays in the mammy's pouch for six months. Then it rides on her back Koalas are lazy little animals. They can sleep for eighteen hours every day.

Using maps and globes, children develop an awareness of people and places in a non-European country and become familiar with some of the aspects of life there.

A - Questions

1 Is Australia an island?

2 Where do most of the people live?

3 Where does Mildred live?

4 Do children in the outback go to a school?

5 What is a doctor in the outback called?

6 What is a baby kangaroo called?

7 What toy does a koala look like?

8 Where does the baby koala stay for six months?

B - The Flying Doctor. Colour the picture.

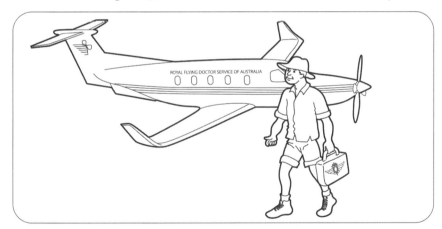

Fast Facts!

- Australia is the largest island in the world.
- There are more than 50 kinds of kangaroos.
- A group of kangaroos is called a mob.

C - Colour. Name the Capital City.

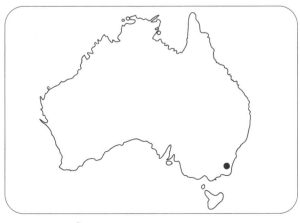

C_____.

Easter Customs

Easter is a special time in spring. People celebrate how Jesus died and rose again.

Eggs are a sign of new life. We eat chocolate eggs at Easter. Long ago, people ate a few boiled eggs for breakfast on Easter Sunday morning. Some eggs were boiled and painted with bright colours.

Egg rolling is an old Easter custom. People rolled eggs down a grassy hill. The person whose egg reached the bottom first was the winner. An egg-rolling contest is held in the garden of the White House, the home of the President of the USA, every year.

In some parts of the world, a parade is held as part of a festival called 'Mardi Gras' (Fat Tuesday). Mardi Gras is always the day before Ash Wednesday, when Lent begins. People celebrate with a party, a parade and fireworks before fasting for Lent. Brazil and the city of New Orleans in the USA are famous for Mardi Gras festivals.

Children explore and discuss the origins and traditions of Easter and discuss traditions and customs in other lands.

A - Talk to an older person about how Easter may have been celebrated in the past.

Write about it.

_____

_____

_____

_____

_____

_____

_____

_____

B - Easter Egg Hunt

Find the eggs in the bush. Colour them.

Aerial Photographs

Photographs of land and sea taken from an aeroplane are called aerial photographs.
Look at these aerial photographs. Discuss.

Children develop their map-reading skills by using aerial photographs.

A - My home

Draw a picture of your home as you would see it from the air.

B - My school

Draw a picture of your school as you would see it from the air.

Barry the Bin Man

Hello! My name is Barry the Bin Man. I have a very busy job. I visit all the houses to collect their rubbish. My truck is ready to burst after collecting everything!

When my truck is full I drive to the landfill. This is a very big hole that we fill with rubbish. It looks and smells very bad. Phew!

I feel very sad when I see all the rubbish we throw away. Most of it could be recycled. When we recycle we can make our rubbish new again. We can recycle glass, plastic, cans and clothes.

Look at these signs on things at home. They mean that you can recycle something instead of throwing it away.

When something is recycled it can have a very different use.

A - Match

See if you can match the rubbish to its new use after it has been recycled.

Rubbish

newspaper

plastic bottle

clothes

glass bottle

New Use

fibreglass boat

cleaning cloth

wellies

toilet paper

B - Sort

Match the rubbish that can be recycled to the correct bin.

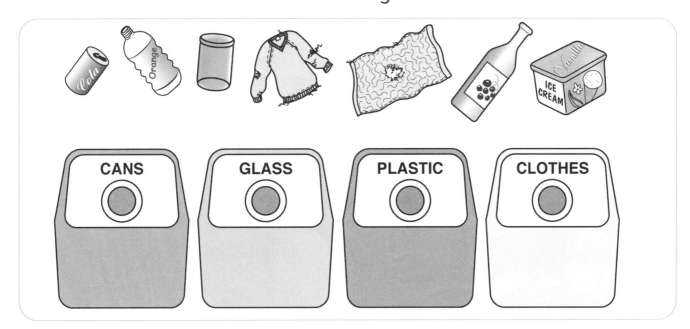

CANS   GLASS   PLASTIC   CLOTHES

C - Poster

Design a poster telling people to recycle their rubbish.

Night and Day

A big spinning top!

The world is always spinning. It will never stop. It takes 24 hours to make one full turn. That is one full day. Our world – Planet Earth – looks like a great, big ball floating in a sky full of stars and other planets.

The sun gives us light. When the sun shines down on us we have daytime. As we turn away from the sun it gets dark. We have night-time. That is why it is daytime in Ireland when it is night-time in Australia.

Falling off the world!

If the world is like a ball why do we not fall off? We do not fall off because a strong force pulls everything towards the centre of the earth. It is called gravity. No matter where we are in the world, gravity keeps us from falling off.

64

Children develop familiarity with Planet Earth through questioning and observing. They explore the differences between day and night.

A - Which do you like best – daytime or night-time?

early   shining   school   friends   play   shopping
playground   bed   story   read   television   sleepy
dark   moon   stars   outside   tired

I like_____ best because_____

_____

_____

_____

_____

_____

_____

_____

B - Draw a picture to show your favourite time of the day or night. Talk about it.

The Giant from Scotland

Long, long ago Fionn and his wife Una lived in Co. Antrim. Their home was by the sea.

> Angus the giant wants to fight you!

> I will fight him.

One day a messenger came from Scotland to speak to Fionn.

Fionn got lots of rocks. He began to build a path across the sea to Scotland.

> What's wrong Una?

> I heard that Angus is bigger and stronger than you.

Fionn saw that Una was sad.

> Here are big baby clothes. Put them on.

> And here is a big cradle.

Angus the giant from Scotland came to the door. Una let him in.

Fionn and Una thought of a plan.

Children listen to, discuss and retell an Irish legend. They may communicate the events of the legend through writing and drama.

7 'If this is Fionn's baby,' said Angus, 'I don't want to see his dad!'

8 Angus ran back to Scotland. He broke Fionn's path so Fionn could not follow him. Part of the path can be seen today. It is called 'The Giant's Causeway'.

A - Questions

1. Where did Fionn and Una live?

2. Who wanted to fight Fionn?

3. What did Fionn begin to build?

4. Why was Una sad?

5. How did Fionn scare the giant?

6. What is Fionn's path called?

B - Over to you!

Some day you might visit the Giant's Causeway.

Use your map to find out where it is.

The Seasons

Spring

Spring is a busy time. The weather gets warmer and many flowers are growing again. The buds on the trees start to grow into new leaves.
The squirrel and hedgehog

wake up from their long winter's sleep. The birds build nests for their eggs. Lambs and piglets are born on the farm.

Summer

Summer has long sunny days. We can play outside more and maybe visit the seaside. The flowers are brightly coloured and the trees have lots of green leaves.
The young birds are ready to leave their nests.
The farmer is busy at work.

Autumn

Autumn has colder weather. The leaves on the trees turn red, orange and brown and start to fall. Many birds fly away to warmer places.
The squirrel and hedgehog gather food for their winter's sleep. Blackberries are ripe and ready for picking.

Children will look for and identify seasonal patterns in plant and animal life.

Winter

In winter many plants and animals are resting. The weather is cold and sometimes it snows. We must wear warm clothes. The trees are bare.

The squirrel and hedgehog are sleeping. Food is scarce and some birds and animals may be hungry.

A - Draw a tree in each season.

spring

summer

autumn

winter

B - Write about your favourite season.

_____

_____

_____

Mighty Mountains

The mountains we see around us are millions of years old. Nearly a quarter of all the land in the world is covered by mountains.

Carrauntoohil is the highest mountain in Ireland. It is near Killarney, Co. Kerry.

This is the butterwort. It has bright, sticky green leaves. The leaves trap insects.

Deer, goats and sheep live on mountains. Many birds live there too. Lots of flowers grow on mountains.

Some mountains are so high that they are covered in snow all winter. People go there to ski and snowboard. We cannot ski in Ireland. We do not get enough snow.

Children identify and discuss aspects of natural features in the environment.

A - Mountains on a map

This is how we draw mountains on a map. ▲▲▲ Are there mountains near where you live? Draw them on the map. Write the name of the mountains.

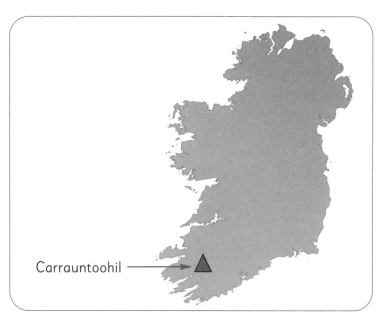

Carrauntoohil →

B - Let's talk!

Mountains can be dangerous. Discuss the pictures.

The Story of Helen Keller

Helen Keller was born in America in 1880. When she was two years old she got sick and became blind and deaf. Five years later, a lady called Anne Sullivan began to teach Helen.

Anne gave Helen a present of a doll. Using her finger, Anne spelled 'doll' on Helen's hand. She poured water on Helen's other hand and spelled 'water'. Helen began to learn how to spell words and give messages to others.

When Helen was nine years old, she learned how to speak. She put her hand on the lips and touched the throat of the person who was talking. That way, she knew what words were being said.

Helen Keller was very brave. She learned to swim, cycle and ride a horse. She went to college. She met the President of the USA in the White House. Helen loved to help others. She visited sick soldiers in hospital. Lots of people came to hear Helen talk about being blind and deaf.

Children explore and discuss Helen Keller's contribution to social, political and health developments.

A - Look inside and outside your school.

List the ways in which you could improve your school to help someone like Helen.

_____

_____

_____

_____

_____

_____

_____

_____

B - Try this!

Anne Sullivan showed Helen lots of words by tracing the letters of the words on Helen's hand. Trace one of these words on your friend's hand. They must keep their eyes shut. See if they can guess which word it is. Then you have a turn.

1 dog   **2** cat   **3** bin   **4** pig   **5** car   **6** cow

Write down four more words that you can trace on your friend's hand.

1 _____   **2** _____

3 _____   **4** _____

The Butterfly

Butterflies are beautiful insects. They have lovely colours and patterns on their wings.

There are many types of butterflies and they are found all over the world.

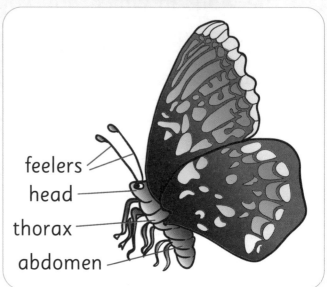

feelers
head
thorax
abdomen

Butterflies like to fly around. They suck the nectar from flowers. A butterfly looked very different when it was born.

Life cycle of a butterfly

1 The butterfly lays her eggs on a leaf.

2 The eggs hatch and a caterpillar crawls out. It is very hungry and eats the leaves on the plant. It eats and eats and soon gets too big for its skin! It sheds its skin and keeps growing.

3 The caterpillar builds a cocoon to hide in. While it is inside it starts to change.

4 After a while the cocoon opens and a beautiful butterfly comes out.

The butterfly leaves the cocoon.

The butterfly lays eggs on a leaf.

Caterpillars eat a lot.

The caterpillar makes a cocoon.

1 _____

2 _____

3 _____

4 _____

B - Look at a book about butterflies.
Draw your favourite pattern.

Windy Days

Wilma Wind

I am Wilma Wind. You cannot see me but you can feel me. I am moving air. You can see what I do. I toss the leaves. I fly flags and kites. I blow the clothes on the line. I whistle through trees. When I am lazy I am a gentle breeze. When I am cross I am a strong gale.

Danger!

Sometimes I travel very fast. I knock down trees and even buildings. Then you call me Horrible Hurricane.

Sometimes I am dizzy and I spin around and around very fast. I can even pull cars and houses up into the air. Then you call me Terrible Tornado.

Wrap up!

When I blow from the east you need your woolly hat and scarf. When I blow from the north I bring snow. Most often I blow from the south and the west. Then you need your umbrella.

Children observe, explore and investigate wind strength. They record the results.

A - Colour the weather vane.

A weather vane tells us the direction wind is blowing from.

B - Write the correct word.

1 Wind is moving _____ . (water, air, ice)

2 A _____ can knock down trees. (hurricane, breeze)

3 A tornado_____around and around. (runs, walks, spins)

4 Wind from the north brings _____ . (snow, sun, heat)

5 Wind from the east is _____ . (hot, warm, cold)

6 A weather vane tells us the direction of_____ .

(rain, wind, sun)

C - My wind diary

Put the correct symbol in the boxes. Write the sentences.

no wind	breeze	windy	very windy

Monday	Tuesday	Wednesday	Thursday	Friday

1 On Monday _____

2 _____

3 _____

4 _____

5 _____

A - Let's talk!

Look at the two photographs. Discuss.

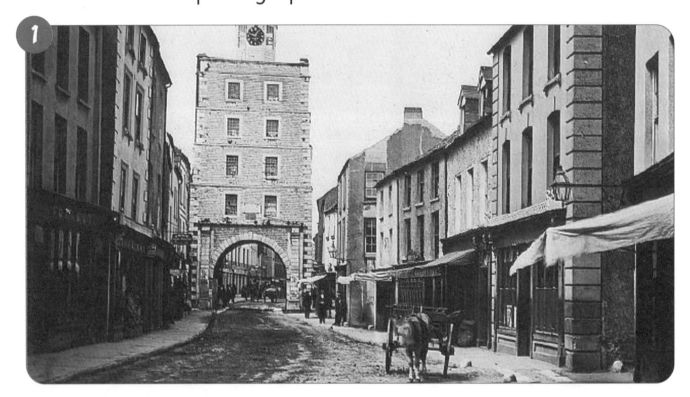

Children identify features of continuity and change by comparing old and new photographs of a town or city.

B - Questions

> houses   shops   arch   windows   clock
> chimney   traffic   signs   streetlight   footpath

1 Write down two things that are the **same** in Photo 1 and Photo 2:

(a) _____

(b) _____

2 Write down two things that are **different** in Photo 1 and Photo 2:

(a) _____

(b) _____

C - Draw a picture on each shop sign.

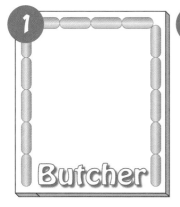
1 Butcher

2 ◈ Mobile Phones ◈

3 CDs & DVDs

4 Bakery

1 Which shop signs would you see today? _____

_____

2 Which shop signs might you have seen long ago? _____

_____

79

Food Chains

All plants and animals need food to give them energy.
Without energy they could not grow. Plants are special.
They can use the energy from the sun to make food.

Animals cannot make their own food.
They must get energy by eating plants
and animals.

Some animals, like the rabbit and the giraffe,
eat plants only. They are called **herbivores**.

Other animals, like the dog and the tiger, eat
meat only. They are called **carnivores**.

There are other animals, like the wolf and the
badger, that eat plants and animals. They are
called **omnivores**.

Food Chains

A food chain is a way of showing how plants
and animals get their energy. A food chain
will start with a plant and end with an animal.

1 grass → rabbit → fox

2 leaves → snail → crow

A - Find the animals that are written in the spiral.

_____   _____
_____   _____
_____   _____
_____   _____

squirreliontigerrabbitwolfgiraffecowdog

B - Now, sort the animals into the correct box.

herbivore	carnivore	omnivore

Tidy Towns Competition

Clara and Ben live in a small town called Killbeg. They like their town very much. They are very proud of it.

Every Saturday, people in the town work together to clean up. Clara, Ben and their friends help too.

They plant flowers, pick up litter and help to make the town clean and tidy.

This year they won the Tidy Towns Competition. They won a medal for the best small town in Ireland. Clara, Ben and all their friends were very, very happy.

Children use their geographical skills to identify and implement strategies to care for and to improve their environment.

A - Read the answer. Write the question.

1 Where _____?
Clara and Ben live in Killbeg.

2 _____?
They work together every Saturday.

3 _____?
They plant flowers.

4 _____?
They pick up litter.

5 _____?
They won a medal.

6 _____?
Yes, they were very happy.

B - Design a poster.

Ask people to keep their area clean and tidy.

C - Let's talk!

What can you do to make where you live look better?

Back to School

A - Let's talk!

Look at the photographs of the classrooms. Discuss.

Children identify features of continuity and change by comparing old and new photographs of schools.

B - Read the story.

'Great-Granny,' said the children. 'Tell us about what school was like when you were a girl.'
'Well,' she said, 'in some ways school was different to nowadays. I didn't have a school uniform. I wore a dress and a cardigan.

In winter, I wore shoes. In summer, my friends and I were allowed to go barefoot! I did a lot of reading, writing and maths. I also learned history and geography.

My schoolbooks did not have many pictures like your schoolbooks. Outside in the yard, I had to do "drill". "Drill" was exercises and marching. Today, you do P.E. at school. The school I went to was small. It had two classrooms.'

'Great-Granny,' said the children, 'we want to go barefoot to school! Please?'
'You are very brave! It's raining outside!' laughed Great-Granny.

C - Read the words in the clouds.

Write them in the correct boxes. Can you think of more words to fill the boxes?

Books with lots of pictures

Drill

P.E.

No shoes – bare feet!

School Today

School Long Ago

Water

Rap – Where would we be without it?

Rain pours down,
We all frown.

But where would we be without it?

All that rain,
It's such a pain.

But where would we be without it?

We all need water
To stay alive,
Without water
We could not survive,
Rivers would dry,
Plants would die.

Where would we be without it?

Water is fun
For everyone,
Swim and float
Or sail a boat,
Splash and dive –
Stay alive!

Where would we be without it?

Children become aware of our dependency on water and its uses.

A - Save our water! Can you think of other ways?

Take a shower instead of a bath.

Do not let water run while you brush your teeth.

B - Write about all the ways you use water.

I use water _____

_____

_____

_____

_____

C - Let's talk!

Water, water everywhere and not a drop to drink!

The Desert

The desert is not a very nice place to live.
It is very hot all day and it gets very cold at night.
It does not rain very often. Many plants cannot grow
in the desert. Only some animals can live there.

Fast Fact!
The largest desert in the world is the Sahara Desert in Africa.

The Saguaro Cactus grows in deserts in the USA and Mexico.

Some plants and animals have adapted to living here.
They have found ways to help them survive.

The camel

Hello! I am Carrie Camel. I love the hot weather in the desert. I hardly ever sweat. I can live without water or food for a whole week. The fat in my hump keeps me going when I get hungry. My thick eyelashes and hairy ears might look funny but they help to keep out the sand.

The cactus

Hello! My name is Cammy Cactus. I like living in the desert too. When it rains I can soak up loads of water. I grow so fat I almost burst! Be careful not to touch me though because I have lots of prickly spines. Ouch!

Children explore, analyse and research animals and plants from a different habitat.

The lizard

Hello! I am Frank the Frilled Lizard. I enjoy the desert sun – it helps to keep me warm. I might look small but I can look very scary when I want to frighten something. I open my mouth really wide and hiss. I spread my frilly neck like an umbrella and it makes me look a lot bigger.

A - Questions

1 What is the weather like in the desert?

_____

2 Where does the camel store its food?

_____

3 Why must you be careful when you touch a cactus?

_____

4 How does the frilled lizard make itself look bigger?

_____

5 Would you like to live in the desert? Why? Why not?

_____

B - Finish the picture.

The Tea Story

I'm a little teapot, Short and stout...

Do you know where tea comes from?

Tea comes all the way from India, China and Sri Lanka. Tea plants grow in big fields called tea plantations. The plants need water and sunshine to grow.

People pick the new leaves at the top of the plants. They put them into baskets. Then they take the leaves to the tea factory.

The leaves are left to wither and dry. Then they are rolled. When the tea is ready it is packed into boxes.

Tea is sold to people all over the world.

Using maps and globes, children recognise and appreciate the interdependence of people at home and in faraway places.

A - Tea comes from India, China and Sri Lanka.

Write the names of the three countries on the map.

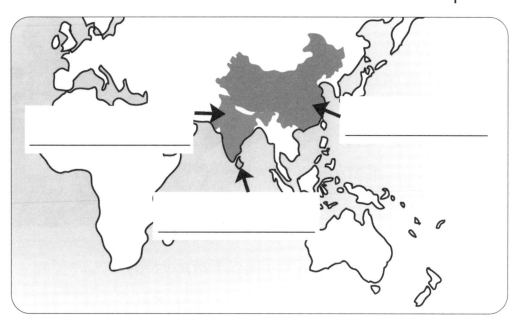

B - Write the story of tea.

grows India tea plantation leaves pick factory wither
dry roll packed sold

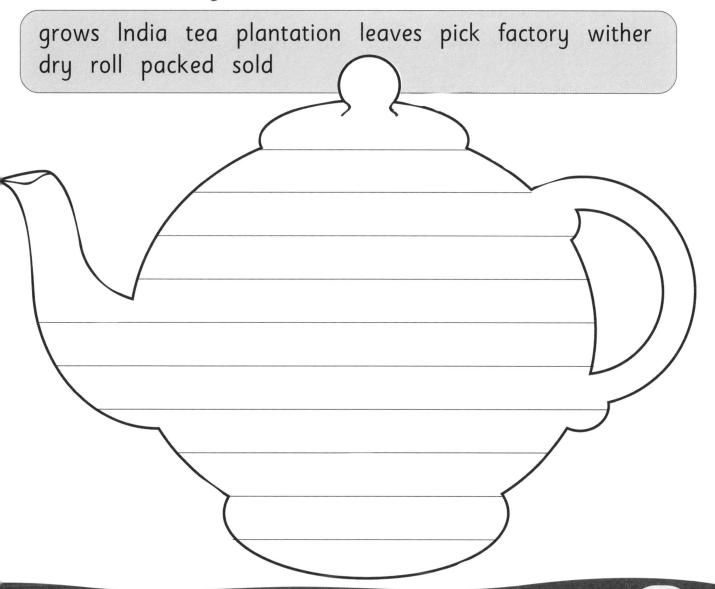

Let's go on a History Trail

It was sunny. The children were very excited. 'We are going on a history trail to the Old Town Hall,' they cheered. 'We will learn lots of things along the way!'

'I have a camera,' said the teacher. 'Have you all got hats and coats in case it rains? You should have a trail book, paper, crayons and a bag to put them all in.'

'Yes,' said the children.

'Ok,' said the teacher. 'Let's go on a history trail!'

The first stop on the trail was at an old gate. The children wrote down the colour of the gate.

Then the children wrote down the name of the street. It was 'Market Street'. 'I wonder why it is called Market Street?' thought Lisa.

Along the way, the children saw a church, an old sweet shop and an old street lamp.

At the town hall, the children wrote down what the walls and roof were made of. They drew a picture of it too. They went inside to explore it.

92

Children examine local evidence to identify instances of change and continuity in the local environment.

'This is very exciting!' said Lisa.
'We have learned lots of things about our town today!' said the children.

A - A history trail

Think about old places or old buildings near your school. If you were going on a history trail, here are some questions to help you.

1. What is the name of the place or building?_____
2. Where did it get its name? _____
3. How old is it?_____
4. Did someone live in it or nearby?_____
5. What was it used for? _____
6. Is it still in use?_____
7. Is there a wall plaque on the building?_____
8. If so, what does it say?_____
9. What does it look like now?_____
10. Did it always look like this?_____
11. Can you learn anything about the lives of the people who lived there in the past?_____
    _____
12. Are there any interesting features?_____
    _____

Look Back

Revision Questions

1 What type of food is at the top of the food pyramid?_____

2 Why is wood used to build houses in very cold countries?_____
_____

3 Why are some houses built on stilts?_____
_____

4 What are people who live in the Arctic called?_____

5 Name a game that Grandad played when he was a boy.
_____

6 What is a gondola?_____

7 What is gelato?_____

8 What did Alexander Graham Bell invent?_____

9 What is glass made from?_____

10 Name a natural material._____

---

1 What is a shantytown?_____

2 Is a window transparent or opaque?_____

3 What did Hasibur's dad bring from Pakistan to Ireland?_____
_____

4 Name one thing Hasibur's sister brought from Pakistan to Ireland.
_____

5 Is there more water or land on Planet Earth?_____

6 At what temperature does water boil?_____

7 How long does Christmas last in The Philippines?_____

8 What is the Christmas procession in Mexico called?_____

9 What is an iceberg?_____

10 What animal has a 3-metre-long tooth?_____

1. Name something in the classroom that uses electricity. _____

_____

2. Where did Queen Maeve and her husband Ailill live? _____

3. What small bird has a red breast? _____

4. What is a joey? _____

5. What is an aerial photograph? _____

6. In 'The Giant from Scotland' what was the giant's name?

_____

7. What is Fionn's path called? _____

8. In which season do birds build nests? _____

9. Name the highest mountain in Ireland. _____

10. What was Helen Keller's teacher called? _____

1. What does a caterpillar become? _____

2. What damage may be caused by a tornado? _____

_____

3. Does a herbivore eat plants or meat? _____

4. What subject did Great-Granny learn at school instead of P.E.?

_____

5. Name two ways to have fun with water. _____

6. Name two reasons why we need water. _____

7. What helps the camel to keep the sand away from its eyes and ears?

_____

8. What is in a camel's hump? _____

9. Name two things the children had to bring on the history trail. _____

_____

10. On the history trail, what was the name of the street that the children
wrote down? _____

Web References

Chpt	Topic	Website Reference
1	All About Me!	http://www.bbc.co.uk/cbeebies/rolymo/library/stories/growingup.shtml
2	Be Healthy!	http://cyh.com/SubDefault.aspx?p=255 http://www.kidshealth.org/misc_pages/mybody_LP.html
3	Sport is Fun	http://www.irishsportscouncil.ie
4	Communications – Old and New	http://inventors.about.com/library/inventors/bl_history_of_communication.htm
5	Good Food	http://www.bordbia.ie/
6	Houses in Far Away Places	http://www.hgpho.to/wfest/house/house-e.html
7	Games from the Past	http://www.learningtogive.org/lessons/unit194/lesson5.html http://www.retrowow.co.uk/retro_britain/toys_and_games/toys_games_past.html
8	Push and Pull	http://my.execpc.com/~rhoadley/magindex.htm
9	Italy	http://www.italiantourism.com/ http://www.euroclubschools.co.uk/page16.htm
10	Alexander Graham Bell	http://www.alexandergrahambell.org/
11	Discover Materials	http://news.bbc.co.uk/2/hi/science/nature/6591649.stm
12	Living in a Box	http://www.svp.ie/
13	Explore Materials	http://www.teacherfiles.com/sharing_science.htm
14	Family Treasures	http://www.tourism.gov.pk/Index.html
15	Planet Earth	http://www.kidsastronomy.com/
16	Heat and temperature	http://id.mind.net/~zona/mstm/physics/mechanics/energy/heatAndTemperature/heatAndTemperature.html
17	Christmas Customs	http://www.soon.org.uk/country/christmas.htm
18	Arctic Weather	http://www3.nationalgeographic.com/places/index.html
19	Shopping Tales	http://www.dunnesstores.ie/page.php?pid=35 http://www.superquinn.ie/ http://www.tesco.ie
20	Electricity	http://www.sciencemadesimple.com/static.html
21	Arctic Animals	http://library.thinkquest.org/3500/
22	Families in the Past	http://www.genwriters.com/children.html
23	Going Outside	http://www.teachers.ash.org.au/jmresources/minibeasts/minibeasts.htm
24	Making Maps	http://www.maps4kids.com/
25	The Brown Bull of Cooley	http://www.shee-eire.com/Magic&Mythology/Myths/Cuchulainn/The-Cattle-raid-of-Cooley-(The-Tain)/page%201.htm
26	Our Feathered Friends	http://www.birdsireland.com/
27	The Land Down Under	http://www.kidport.com/RefLib/WorldGeography/Australia/Australia.htm
28	Easter Customs	http://www.woodlands-junior.kent.sch.uk/customs/easter/
29	Aerial Photographs	http://www.irelandaerialphotography.com/
30	Barry the Bin Man	http://www.citizensinformation.ie/categories/environment/waste-management-and-recycling/domestic_refuse
31	Night and Day	http://www.die.net/earth/
32	The Giant from Scotland	http://en.wikipedia.org/wiki/Fionn_mac_Cumhaill
33	The Seasons	http://csep10.phys.utk.edu/astr161/lect/time/seasons.html
34	Mighty Mountains	http://mountainviews.ie/ http://www.kerrymountainrescue.ie
35	The Story of Helen Keller	http://www.afb.org/braillebug/helen_keller_bio.asp
36	The Butterfly	http://butterflywebsite.com/
37	Windy Days	http://www.first-school.ws/activities/onlinestory/animals/spotwindyday.htm
38	A Town through Time	http://www.dublinuncovered.net/history.html
39	Food Chains	http://www.vtaide.com/png/foodchains.htm
40	Tidy Towns Competition	http://www.tidytowns.ie/
41	Back to School	http://www.schooldays.ie/
42	Water	http://ga.water.usgs.gov/edu/
43	The Desert	http://www.ucmp.berkeley.edu/exhibits/biomes/deserts.php
44	The Tea Story	http://www.superluminal.com/cookbook/essay_tea.html
45	Let's go on a History Trail	http://www.bbc.co.uk/history/trail/